Make a New Friend

PassAlong Arch® Books h[...]
Jesus with friends close to y[...]
children all around the world!

When you've enjoyed this story, pass it
along to a friend.   When your friend is fin-
ished, mail this book to the address below. Concordia Gospel
Outreach promises to deliver your book to a boy or girl some-
where in the world to help him or her learn about Jesus.

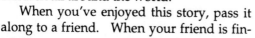

Myself

My name　＿＿＿＿＿＿＿＿＿＿＿＿＿＿＿＿＿＿＿

My address　＿＿＿＿＿＿＿＿＿＿＿＿＿＿＿＿＿＿

　　　　　　＿＿＿＿＿＿＿＿＿＿＿＿＿＿＿＿＿＿

My PassAlong Friend

My name　＿＿＿＿＿＿＿＿＿＿＿＿＿＿＿＿＿＿＿

My address　＿＿＿＿＿＿＿＿＿＿＿＿＿＿＿＿＿＿

　　　　　　＿＿＿＿＿＿＿＿＿＿＿＿＿＿＿＿＿＿

When you're ready to give
your PassAlong Arch® Book to a
new friend who doesn't know
about Jesus, mail it to

Concordia Gospel Outreach
3547 Indiana Avenue
St. Louis, MO 63118

PassAlong Series

God's Good Creation
Noah's Floating Zoo
Baby Moses' River Ride
Moses and the Freedom Flight
Jonah's Fishy Adventure
Daniel in the Dangerous Den
Baby Jesus, Prince of Peace
Jesus Stills the Storm
Jesus and Jairus' Little Girl
Jesus' Big Picnic
God's Easter Plan
Peter and the Biggest Birthday

Copyright © 1995 Concordia Publishing House
3558 S. Jefferson Avenue, St. Louis, MO 63118-3968
Manufactured in the United States of America

1 2 3 4 5 6 7 8 9 10   04 03 02 01 00 99 98 97 96 95

Jesus and Jairus' Little Girl

Matthew 9:18–26, Mark 5:21–43 Luke 8:41–56 for children

Carol Greene
Illustrated by Michelle Dorenkamp

SAINT LOUIS

What did He do, this Jesus man?
What was His Father's holy plan?
Tell us, disciples. Tell and show
One day with Jesus here below.

We'll help you see the Jesus man.
You'll watch Him show the world
    God's plan.
We'll share with you one sunny day.
Ready? Well, let's be on our way.

"How exciting!"

*C*lunk! goes the boat. We've come ashore.
See people gather, more and more.
Hear how the air with voices hums.
That's how it is when Jesus comes.

"Help, Lord!" "Oh, Jesus, please help me."
"I cannot walk." "I cannot see."
Look how He loves them, every one.
Our day with Him has just begun.

"I think it will be a day full of love."

Here's a religious leader, who
Is called Jairus, pushing through.
What's brought him out in all this heat?
He's fallen there at Jesus' feet!

In front of everyone he's crying.
"My only little girl is dying.
But, Jesus, I am positive,
If You just touch her, she will live."

"Poor Jairus!
Poor little girl!"

See Jesus' eyes. He's hurting too.
Although He knows what He can do,
It hurts Him when His friends feel pain.
Still, He will make things right again.

There He goes now to see the child.
We must stay close. This crowd is wild.
They bump our bodies, smush our toes.
That's how it is where Jesus goes.

Now Jesus stops. "Who touched My clothes?"
"With all these people, Lord, who knows?
From every side they push and press.
Who touched You, we can only guess."

Still Jesus looks. He seems to feel
That touch was different, far more real,
Or strong, or something, than the rest.
He's looking . . . ah! Here comes the pest.

"I didn't do it!"

Why, it's a woman! See her shake.
She's weak from fear for her mistake.
She's fallen at the Lord's feet too.
But what exactly did she do?

"I touched You, Lord. Hear, if You will,"
She says. "For twelve years I've been ill.
I've been to doctors far and near
And just got worse. So I came here."

"Twelve long years!"

Some people told me who You were,
But I could not get to You, Sir.
No one could hear me if I spoke,
So I reached out and touched Your cloak.

"That's all I want, Lord, all I need.
One simple touch and now I'm freed
From suffering and sadness too.
I'm well, my Lord, because of You."

"Now that's really something."

Is Jesus angry? Does He mind?
Why, no. His words are gentle, kind.
"Your faith has brought you this release.
Be well, My daughter. Go in peace."

But look! Some men have come from town,
Their faces twisted in a frown.
"Move over there." "Get back." "Make way!"
"We've brought Jairus news," they say.

"This looks bad."

What news?" Jairus asked with dread.
"Bad news. Your little girl is dead.
Let this mob go back to the shore.
Don't bother Jesus anymore."

But Jesus doesn't seem to hear.
"Come on, Jairus. Do not fear."
He tugs the poor man's dusty sleeve.
"Come on, Jairus, Just believe.

"Listen to Jesus, Jairus!"

The rest of you will have to stay.
Just Peter, James, and John today
May go along," says Jesus. "Come,
Take us, Jairus, to your home."

So on we go. We don't know why
Unless it is to wail and cry
With all the other mourners there,
To show Jairus that we care.

Listen to flutes play their sad song;
Then mourners' wails. They're loud
    and strong.
"Why do you fuss and fret and weep?
That child's not dead. She's just asleep."

At Jesus' words, they laugh and jeer.
"How would You know? You weren't here.
She's dead, all right, and dead she'll stay.
We plan to mourn like this all day."

"You folks just wait and see!"

Then Jesus looks them in the eye.
"Out, now!" He says, and out they fly.
You'd think by now these folks would know
Not to doubt Jesus. Up we go!

Up with her parents to her room,
Chilly and silent as a tomb.
There on the bed the young girl lies.
Surely it's death that closed her eyes.

Jesus goes over, takes her hand.
"*Talitha koum*, young maiden, stand!"
And stand she does, and walks around.
That child is healthy, strong, and sound!

"What have You done?" her parents gasp,
As both their daughter's hands they clasp.
But they can't stop her busy feet.
Jesus smiles. "Give her food to eat."

Don't tell a soul about all this,"
Jesus says. But that small miss,
Dancing for joy in her new day,
Tells more than any words can say.

And that's *our* day. The sun goes down.
Jesus will leave for His hometown.
Now you have seen the Jesus man
Living His Father's holy plan.

"What a day!"

That plan is life, for you, for me,
Life to be lived abundantly.
From death's sad sleep, He's set *us* free.
Now do you know? Now do you see?

"What a plan!"